CONVERSATIONS WITH LEGENDS

Being A Blessing While I Can

Created by Linda Morgan Sam

Volume 1: Aaron "Taco" Sam

KP PUBLISHING COMPANY

Conversations with Legends – Aaron "Taco" Sam

ISBN: 979-8-995314-50-9 (Paperback)
ISBN: 979-8-995314-51-6 (eBook)

Library of Congress Control Number: Pending

Published by:

KP Publishing Company
Publisher of Fiction, Nonfiction & Children's Books
Las Vegas, NV 89117
www.kp-pub.com

Printed in the United States of America

DEDICATION

This volume is dedicated to our honored
Legends who graced the stage, the page, and our lives,
and have now gone home to glory.

We celebrate you not in silence,
but in rhythm, remembrance, and resolve.

The song you started still plays.
The words you lived still speak.
The doors you opened remain wide.

Thank you for showing us how to live boldly, create fearlessly,
and leave something worthy behind.

Legends never leave.
They simply change rooms.

“TRUE LEGENDS WALK BY FAITH,
LEAD WITH PURPOSE,
AND LEAVE FOOTPRINTS THAT
TIME CANNOT ERASE.”

FOREWORD

Conversations with Legends is a preservation of living history. Within these pages are voices that have shaped culture, strengthened communities, and left indelible marks on the world through purpose and perseverance.

I have had the privilege of mentoring Linda Morgan Sam and witnessing her deep respect for legacy and storytelling. She approaches each conversation with intention, listening not only for achievements, but for lessons meant to be passed forward. This work reflects her understanding that stories are sacred and that honoring our legends while they can still speak is both timely and necessary.

These conversations remind us that greatness is forged through discipline, faith, creativity, and service. They offer wisdom for the present and guidance for generations to come.

May this series inspire you to honor the past, walk boldly in your calling, and leave a meaningful legacy of your own.

With admiration,
Dr. Barbara A. Perkins

"WHAT MAKES A LEGEND
IS NOT FAME, BUT THE COURAGE
TO LIVE A LIFE WORTH
REMEMBERING AND REPEATING."

CONTENTS

Publisher's Note

At KP Publishing, we believe that every life carries a story worth preserving.

The *Conversations with Legends* series was created to honor individuals whose journeys have shaped their communities, influenced others, and left lasting impressions through their gifts, talents, and service. These are the voices that often go unrecorded, yet they hold wisdom that can guide generations.

This inaugural volume, featuring Aaron "Taco" Sam, represents the heart of this series.

Taco's life is a reflection of what it means to live with purpose, passion, and consistency. His love for music, his appreciation for harmony, and his deep commitment to family and faith remind us that legacy is not built solely on recognition, but on the lives we touch along the way.

Through this book, we are not only preserving his story, we are celebrating a life that continues to inspire.

It is our hope that readers will not only enjoy these conversations, but also be encouraged to recognize the legends in their own lives and take the time to preserve their stories.

Because when we honor the voices of today, we create a foundation for tomorrow.

Willa Robinson
Legacy Builder & Publisher
KP Publishing Company

WHY WE MUST PRESERVE OUR LEGENDS

Every generation is shaped by the lives and voices of those who came before it.

Some sang the songs that lifted our spirits. Some told the stories that helped us understand who we are. Others lived their lives with such faith, resilience, and purpose that their example became a guiding light for everyone around them.

These are the individuals we call legends.

Yet too often, their stories are never fully recorded.

Their wisdom is shared in conversations at kitchen tables, on front porches, in church pews, and within communities, but rarely written down. Over time, those stories fade, and the lessons they carried risk being lost.

Preserving the stories of our legends is not simply about honoring the past. It is about strengthening the future.

Their journeys reveal the truth behind success: the sacrifices, the perseverance, the discipline, and the faith required to overcome life's challenges. They remind us that greatness is not accidental. It is built over time through commitment, character, and courage.

When we take the time to listen, to document, and to share these stories, we create a bridge between generations.

We give future readers the opportunity to learn from real lives, to be inspired by real experiences, and to understand that their own journey has meaning and purpose.

The Conversations with Legends series was created with this mission in mind: to capture these voices while they can still be heard, and to preserve them in a way that will continue to inspire for years to come.

Because every legend carries a story worth telling.

And every story preserved becomes a gift to the generations that follow.

WHAT MAKES A LEGEND?

A legend is not defined only by fame or recognition.

A legend is someone whose life leaves a lasting imprint on others.

Legends are people who dedicate themselves to their craft, their calling, or their community. They face challenges, make sacrifices, and continue moving forward even when the path is uncertain.

Often, legends do not see themselves that way. They simply follow their passion, live their values, and remain committed to what matters most.

Over time, their actions inspire others. Their stories become lessons. Their lives become examples of perseverance, creativity, and faith.

The individuals featured in the *Conversations with Legends* series remind us that greatness is not always found in headlines or applause.

Sometimes it is found in a lifetime of dedication.

And the legacy that follows.

Legend Profile Aaron "Taco" Sam

(AIR-uhn "TAH-koh")

Singing, Harmonizing, and Living a Life of Love

Aaron "Taco" Sam is a man whose life has been shaped by music, grounded in family, and guided by faith.

Born with a natural love for sound and expression, Taco's journey into music began at an early age when his mother recognized something special in him. At just eight years old, she purchased a piano—an act that would quietly set the course for his life. What began as curiosity soon became passion, and that passion grew into purpose.

From childhood into adulthood, Taco has remained connected to music in its purest form: singing, playing, and most of all, harmonizing. For him, music has never been just about performance. It has always been about connection. The blending of voices, the sharing of emotion, and the unity created through song have defined his musical experience.

Over the years, Taco's journey led him to moments that many aspiring artists only dream of. Among those experiences was the opportunity to perform with the legendary R&B group, The Delfonics.

The Delfonics were one of the most influential soul groups of the late 1960s and 1970s, known for their smooth harmonies, heartfelt lyrics, and timeless sound. With classic songs such as "La-La (Means I Love You)" and "Didn't I (Blow Your Mind This Time)," they helped define an era of music that continues to inspire artists today.

To share space with a group of that caliber was not only an honor, but also a powerful moment in Taco's journey. It offered him a glimpse into the discipline, excellence, and artistry required to sustain a life in music.

Yet even with such experiences, Taco's life has never been defined by recognition alone.

What sets him apart is his consistency, his steady commitment to his gift, his love for people, and his unwavering faith. Through every season of life, music has remained a thread that connects his past to his present.

Beyond the stage, Taco's greatest pride is found in his family. As a husband and father of five children: four sons and one daughter, he considers his role within his family to be his most meaningful accomplishment.

Those who know Taco best describe him as a man of warmth, humility, and deep love for others. Whether through music, conversation, or simple presence, he has a way of bringing people together.

His message, carried through both his life and his music, is clear and enduring:

Love one another.

Today, as he continues to sing and reflect on a lifetime of experiences, Taco Sam stands as a reminder that a life lived with purpose does not require fame to be meaningful.

It requires a heart.

And through his voice, his relationships, and his unwavering spirit, Aaron "Taco" Sam has created a legacy that will continue to resonate for generations to come.

"TACO" MORE THAN A NICKNAME

Growing up in San Pedro, California, Aaron spent much of his time in a vibrant Mexican community where many of his friends spoke fluent Spanish.

Those friendships came naturally to him. There was no divide, only connection, laughter, and shared experiences.

Aaron didn't see differences. He saw people. But one day, everything shifted in a small but meaningful way.

As Aaron walked into his high school alongside his Spanish-speaking friends, a group of his African American friends noticed and questioned him.

"Why are you with them?"

The question carried more than curiosity. It reflected a moment of cultural misunderstanding, something Aaron had not considered before.

His response was simple, sincere, and without hesitation:

"I love them. They're my friends."

There was no explanation beyond that. No need to justify what, to him, felt completely natural.

From that moment on, his friends gave him a nickname that would stay with him for the rest of his life:

"Taco."

What began as a lighthearted label quickly became a name spoken with familiarity, recognition, and over time, respect.

Today, the name Aaron "Taco" Sam is known and embraced by friends, fellow musicians, and audiences alike. It is more than a nickname, it is a reflection of connection, cultural appreciation, and the kind of openness that has defined his life.

And like the harmony he loves so deeply, it all began with simply bringing people together.

ROOTS THAT SHAPED HIM

Aaron "Taco" Sam's journey is rooted in a rich blend of places, experiences, and cultural influences that helped shape the man he would become.

"Louisiana to Philly and then growing up in San Pedro and Los Angeles," he explains.

Each of these places contributed something unique to his life. From the deep cultural and musical traditions of Louisiana to the vibrant energy of Philadelphia, and finally to the diverse communities of Southern California, Taco was surrounded by a variety of sounds, people, and experiences that would leave a lasting impression on him.

But beyond geography, the true foundation of his life was built on something deeper.

Music.

From an early age, music was not just something Taco heard, it was something he felt. It was present in the environments around him, in the communities he was part of, and in the rhythm of everyday life. Whether through church, neighborhood gatherings, or personal exploration, music became a constant thread woven through his experiences.

Entertainment, creativity, and expression were not distant ideas. They were part of his world.

And as he grew, so did his understanding of his place within it.

By the time he was about 12 years old, Taco came to a realization that would guide the rest of his life:

"This is my gift. This is what I'm meant to do."

It was not a moment of uncertainty, but one of clarity.

He recognized that music was more than a hobby, it was a calling.

And from that point forward, everything he experienced, every place he lived, and every person he encountered became part of the journey that would shape his sound, his voice, and his purpose.

THE EARLY JOURNEY

Like many artists, Aaron "Taco" Sam's journey into music was not defined by a single moment, but by a series of experiences that gradually shaped his path.

As his passion for music continued to grow, so did his opportunities to explore it. What began in childhood as curiosity and enjoyment started to take on greater meaning. Taco was no longer just discovering music, he was beginning to live it.

One of the defining moments in his early journey came when he had the opportunity to perform with the well-known R&B group, The Delfonics.

For any young artist, sharing space with an established and respected group is both exciting and formative. The Delfonics, known for their smooth harmonies and timeless sound, represented a level of excellence that Taco admired. Being around that level of artistry offered him more than just exposure, it gave him insight.

He saw firsthand the discipline required to perform at a high level. He experienced the importance of preparation, professionalism, and consistency. And perhaps most importantly, he witnessed what it meant to truly connect with an audience through music.

That experience became part of his foundation.

But Taco's journey was not built on talent alone.

What sustained him through the early stages of his path was something deeper, his faith, his family, and his connection to church.

"My faith in God, my family, and attending church kept me going," he says. "I just enjoyed it all."

There was joy in the journey.

Not pressure. Not performance for recognition. But a genuine love for the gift he had been given.

And that love became the fuel that carried him forward.

As his early journey unfolded, Taco continued to grow, not only as a musician, but as a person. Each experience added to his understanding of his calling, and each step brought him closer to fully embracing the life he was meant to live.

THE JOY OF THE CRAFT

Ask Aaron "Taco" Sam what he loves most about music, and his answer comes without hesitation.

"Harmonizing when singing with others," he says, placing his hand over his heart. "I just love that."

For Taco, music has never been only about performance. It has always been about connection.

There is something deeply meaningful to him about voices coming together, each one different, yet blending to create a single, unified sound. Harmony, in its purest form, represents more than music. It reflects a sense of togetherness, a shared experience that cannot be created alone.

When voices align in harmony, something happens that goes beyond technique.

It becomes a feeling.

It becomes an expression.

It becomes something that reaches people in ways words alone cannot.

For Taco, those moments are where the true joy of music lives.

It is not about being seen.

It is not about recognition or applause.

It is about the experience of creating something beautiful with others, something that can be felt as much as it is heard.

That joy has remained with him throughout his life.

Whether singing on a stage, in a church, or simply among friends, Taco finds fulfillment in the act of sharing his gift. Each note, each harmony, each moment of connection reminds him why he fell in love with music in the first place.

And even after all these years, that feeling has never faded.

It has only grown stronger.

JazzZone JazZabration
Congratulations on being selected to receive
the Living Legend Award
JazzZone
JazZabration
JazzZone
JazZabration
Tony Taco Sam
Friday, June 30, 2023 | 6pm-10pm
Lavender Blue
3310 W. Manchester Ave.
Inglewood, CA 90302

City of Los Angeles
Certificate of Recognition
is hereby presented to
Aaron Sam
Vocalist (Delfonics), Living Legend Award
In recognition of your many years of contributions to the world of Music. Your passion and mission to ensure that Good Music continues to live on in the hearts and minds of current and future generations are truly commendable. We join the Black Business Association, JazzZone JazzAmerica, Inc., and the Lorce Rose Grooves, celebrating the June 2023 Black Music Month Living Legend Awards while congratulating you for becoming a Living Legend. Best wishes for continued success in all your future endeavors.
June 2023
HEATHER HUTT
Councilmember 10th District
KAREN BASS
Mayor
MARQUEECE HARRIS-DAWSON
Councilmember 8th District
CURREN D. PRICE, JR.
Councilmember 9th District

THE PRICE OF A CALLING

Every calling comes with a cost.

For Aaron "Taco" Sam, the journey of music, while filled with joy and purpose, also required sacrifice.

"It cost my time, relationships, sleep, comfort, and all the rest," he says.

There is a quiet honesty in that statement.

Behind every moment of harmony, every performance, and every opportunity to share his gift, there were choices that had to be made. Time spent developing his craft meant time away from other things. Pursuing his passion required discipline, focus, and a willingness to give up comfort for growth.

Like many who follow their calling, Taco understood that purpose often demands more than talent.

It demands commitment.

There were long days and late nights. Moments when rest had to wait. Times when relationships were tested by the demands of his journey. These are the parts of a calling that are not always seen, but they are very real.

Yet even with all that it required, Taco never lost sight of why he began.

After a brief pause, he adds something that speaks to the heart of his journey:

"But it was worth the price."

Not because the path was easy, but because it was meaningful.

For Taco, the sacrifices were never greater than the purpose they served. Each challenge, each moment of giving more than was convenient, became part of the story that shaped his life.

And in the end, the cost of the calling became part of the reward.

Because when a person walks in what they were created to do, even the sacrifices carry value.

THE LOVE THAT CARRIED HIM

No journey is ever traveled alone.

Behind every step forward, there are often people whose love, support, and belief make the path possible. For Aaron "Taco" Sam, that support came from two women who have been pillars in his life.

His mother, and his wife, Linda Sam.

It was his mother who first recognized the gift within him. When she placed a piano in front of him at just eight years old, she did more than give him an instrument. She gave him an opportunity. She saw something in her son and nurtured it, planting a seed that would grow into a lifelong calling.

That kind of belief leaves a lasting imprint.

It creates confidence. It creates direction. And in many ways, it becomes the foundation for everything that follows.

Years later, as Taco continued to walk in his purpose, another source of strength stood beside him, his wife, Linda.

"Linda has been there for me in every way possible," he says.

Her presence has been more than supportive. It has been sustaining. Through the demands of life, the sacrifices required by his calling, and the many seasons of his journey, she has remained a constant source of encouragement and partnership.

Together, these two women represent something deeply important in Taco's life:

Support that never wavered.

Love that remained steady.

And belief that helped carry him forward.

Because while talent may open doors, it is often the people who stand beside us who help us walk through them.

WHAT MATTERS MOST

When asked what he is most proud of, something that may not always be recognized or applauded, Aaron "Taco" Sam does not mention music, performances, or accomplishments.

Instead, he smiles.

And his answer comes with unmistakable pride: "My children. Four boys and one girl."

In that moment, it becomes clear that Taco's greatest legacy is not found on a stage.

It is found at home.

Beyond the music, beyond the years of dedication to his craft, it is his role as a father that he holds closest to his heart. The lives he has helped shape, the love he has given, and the example he has set mean more to him than any recognition he could receive.

Family, to Taco, is not separate from his journey, it is the center of it.

It is where his values are lived out.

It is where his love is most deeply expressed.

And it is where his legacy will continue long after the music fades.

Because in the end, what matters most is not what we achieve.

It is who we love.

And who we leave behind to carry that love forward.

WISDOM FOR THE NEXT GENERATION

After decades of music, life experience, and personal growth, Aaron "Taco" Sam has learned many lessons along the way.

But when asked what he would share with the next generation, his message is not complicated.

It is not long.

It is not filled with instructions or conditions.

It is simple. "Love one another."

There is a quiet power in those words.

In a world that often feels divided, fast-paced, and uncertain, Taco's message calls us back to something foundational, something that has the power to bring people together, just as music does.

To love one another is to show kindness, to extend grace, and to treat others with respect and understanding. It is to see beyond differences and recognize the shared humanity that connects us all.

It is the same spirit that shaped his friendships, influenced his music, and guided the way he has lived his life.

And while the message may be simple, its impact is profound.

Because when love becomes the foundation, everything else begins to fall into place.

Taco does not just offer this as advice. He has lived it. And now, he passes it forward.

IT'S NEVER TOO LATE

Even now, Aaron "Taco" Sam continues to sing, share his gift, and find joy in the music that has been a part of his life for decades.

Time has not diminished his passion.

If anything, it has deepened it.

"I'll be 80 later than ever," he says with a smile. "When I sing, I can feel the sound of Luther Vandross and many of the greats."

There is something powerful in that statement.

It speaks not only to his love for music, but to the way it continues to live within him. The voices that inspired him, the sounds that shaped him, and the experiences he has gathered over the years are still present every time he sings.

Music, for Taco, is not something that belongs to the past.

It is something that continues to move through him. And with that comes a message that reaches far beyond his own life:

"It's never too late."

Never too late to embrace your gift.

Never too late to pursue what you love.

Never too late to become who you were created to be.

Taco's life stands as a reminder that purpose does not have an expiration date. The desire to create, to share, and to grow does not fade with time, it evolves.

And as long as there is breath, there is still something meaningful to give.

A PORCH-SWING BLESSING

You were sitting with Aaron "Taco" Sam on a quiet front porch swing, with time slowed down and nothing pressing to pull you away, his words would not be complicated.

They would be simple.

They would be sincere.

And they would come from the heart.

"Always love one another, especially family."

There is a calmness in that kind of wisdom. It does not rush.

It does not demand attention.

It simply settles in, like a gentle reminder of what truly matters.

After a lifetime of music, relationships, experiences, and lessons learned, Taco's message comes back to the same place it has always been:

Love.

Not just in words, but in action.

Not just in moments, but in a way of living. It is the kind of love that holds families together, that bridges differences, and that creates a foundation strong enough to carry us through every season of life.

And as the conversation fades and the porch swing slows, that message remains.

Simple.

Steady.

Enduring.

Because in the end, the greatest blessing we can give and the greatest legacy we can leave, is love.

ABOUT THE AUTHOR

Linda Morgan Sam

Linda Morgan Sam is a storyteller, visionary, and passionate advocate for preserving the voices and legacies of those who have shaped culture, community, and generations of lived experience.

As the creator of the *Conversations with Legends* series, she is dedicated to capturing the stories of remarkable individuals whose journeys offer wisdom, inspiration, and guidance for future generations. Through thoughtful conversations and reflective storytelling, Linda brings to life the experiences of those whose contributions might otherwise go unrecorded.

Her work is rooted in a deep respect for legacy and a belief that every life holds lessons worth sharing.

This inaugural volume, featuring Aaron "Taco" Sam, reflects her commitment to honoring stories that matter, stories of faith, perseverance, creativity, and love.

Linda believes that preserving these voices not only honors the past, but helps shape the future.

Linda resides in Nevada with her husband, Aaron "Taco" Sam.

www.ingramcontent.com/pod-product-compliance
Ingram Content Group UK Ltd.
Pitfield, Milton Keynes, MK11 3LW, UK
UKHW062257290726
14090UKWH00017B/746

9 798995 31450